XANADU

SIMON ARMITAGE

Xanadu

BLOODAXE BOOKS

Copyright © Simon Armitage 1992

ISBN: 1 85224 158 6

First published 1992 by
Bloodaxe Books Ltd,
P.O. Box 1SN,
Newcastle upon Tyne NE99 1SN.

Bloodaxe Books Ltd acknowledges
the financial assistance of Northern Arts.

LEGAL NOTICE
All rights reserved. No part of this book may be
reproduced, stored in a retrieval system, or
transmitted in any form, or by any means, electronic,
mechanical, photocopying, recording or otherwise,
without prior written permission from Bloodaxe Books Ltd.
Requests to publish work from this book
must be sent to Bloodaxe Books Ltd.
The video stills are reproduced by kind permission of
Words on Film, BBC Television Features Department, Bristol.

Video stills by Newland Electronics, Newcastle upon Tyne.

Cover reproduction by V & H Reprographics, Newcastle upon Tyne.

Cover printing by J. Thomson Colour Printers, Glasgow.

Printed in Great Britain by
Bell & Bain Limited, Glasgow, Scotland.

XANADU
A poem film by SIMON ARMITAGE

PHOTOGRAPHY	Colin Clarke
	Chris Sugden-Smith
SOUND RECORDIST	David Keene
	Chris Atkinson
PRODUCTION ASSISTANT	Suzie Sampson
UNIT MANAGER	Valerie Mitchell
ASSISTANT PRODUCER	Julia Simmons
GRAPHIC DESIGNER	Sarah Grigg
DUBBING MIXER	Neil Hipkiss
FILM EDITOR	Martin Elsbury
	Angela Groves
EXECUTIVE PRODUCER	Peter Symes
POET	Simon Armitage
FIRST TRANSMISSION	*Words on Film*, BBC-2, June 1992
	BBC Bristol © 1991
FIRST PUBLICATION	Bloodaxe Books, April 1992

Do you copy? Do you read me, over?

Last night I dreamt
I went to Manderley again,
unravelled the thread
of the drive, meandered again

between the buildings
high and dark on either side
until the moon rolled in,
and at its beam

the drive ran into silver
like a silver stream
and brought the brickwork
out of hiding. There it stood:

the architecture breaking cover,
the terrace, the lawns,
the turrets, those windows,
the line of the stream

running out to sea. To Manchester
and its great armada;
each house a boat,
each street a tanker,

each streetlight passing
for a buoy or lantern,
land ahoy,
every cloud a mountain.

But this is midnight
and moonshine plays a cheap trick
on the skyline,
on the eyesight.

Dawn comes like a thaw
and in more natural light
we see this land,
this place. What is it?...

mischief, sorcery,
moonlight, mockery,
makes up and takes
this scene for Manderley,

equates this plot
with that estate,
mistakes the two,
trips up the memory,

reads Ashfield Valley
as Daphne du Maurier.

I was
a probation officer raring to go,
a recently qualified fresh-faced P.O.,
on standby, on hold, awaiting the order
and the call-up posted me over the border,

to Rochdale.
The six things I knew about Rochdale, I'll list them:
a football team in the fourth division,
a famous bridge of considerable width,
home of the Co-op and Cyril Smith,
the pitch of Gracie Fields singing 'Sally,
Sally, pride of our alley',

and a housing estate called Ashfield Valley,
a maze of a place I'd once heard said
had twenty-six blocks labelled A to Z.

A for Appleby,
B for Buttermere,
C for Crosshill,
get the picture?

C for Crosshill,
D for Dunblane,
E for Elsdon,
and so on, and so on.

E for Elsdon
etc etc,
all the way through
to Z for Zennor.

So,
I was a rookie,
just out of college,
finding my feet,
out of my league,

new to probation
when a friend or colleague
turned my head
with some common knowledge:

'Take care when you walk
in the shadow of the Valley.
A fist of keys
and a torch would be handy

and bones for the dogs
at the end of each landing.
A map would be good,
not to read but to shred

and drop out behind
like pieces of bread,
and a finger of chalk
to mark out a thread.

Keep to the path,
whistle in the dark,
don't park in the car park
and never look back.

Picture this: butcher, baker,
Theseus, Hansel, Mercury, Orpheus,
Home Office, Welfare, Probation Service...
you name it, as I walked next night

through the streets in the sky,
heart in my mouth,
to deliver by hand
a summons to a man

with a hell of a past.
This place beyond me,
the hour ungodly,
bearing in mind

not a word of advice
but a word like a knife
from the wise to the rookie:
unlucky.

You said in your sleep
we should blaze our way

from that basement flat
on Memory Lane

to a place in the country
we'd set our hearts on;

I tipped the petrol
but they called it arson,

and being my man
you carried the can

for eighteen months
at Her Majesty's Pleasure

in the Strangeway's Hotel,
and sent me this letter:

Not the ounce of snout
but the smell of the cabbage,

not the slopping out
but the smell of the cabbage,

not the landing light
but the smell of the cabbage,

not the Governor's wife
but the smell of the cabbage.

Not the petty cash
but the smell of the cabbage,

not the forearm smash
but the smell of the cabbage,

not the arm of the law
but the smell of the cabbage,

not the foot in the door
but the smell of the cabbage.

Not the hospital tuck
but the smell of the cabbage,

not the five-knuckle-fuck
but the smell of the cabbage,

not the Spanish guitar
but the smell of the cabbage,

not the budgerigar
but the smell of the cabbage.

Not the bird, the stretch,
the term, the porridge

but the sound of the town
and the smell of the cabbage,

not the girl, the wife,
the woman, the marriage

but the sun going down
and the smell of the cabbage.

Not the file in the cake
but the smell of the cabbage,

not The Great Escape
but the smell of the cabbage,

not the men on the roof
but the smell of the cabbage,

not the truth, the whole truth
but the smell of the cabbage.

Not the night on the block
but the smell of the cabbage,

not the light through the lock
but the smell of the cabbage,

not the eighteen months,
but the criminal damage,

and the smell of the cabbage,
and the smell of the cabbage.

A million books
don't make it clearer,
a thousand years
and we're still no nearer.

All that guff
about place and space,
an ocean of stuff
and it's still a case

of ip dip dip,
my blue ship,
which came first

the flea or the pit?
Which makes which,
the pig or the sty?
All that time

and we're still not certain,
what wears what,
the brick or the person?

This shower of ringdoves has found a home
on the windowsills of these pigeonholes,

and a single magpie is here to stay,
one for sorrow, like a weather vane.

But never a call from the squadron of swallows
that shows up in April, towing the summer,

and never a chance of the fortune they lend
to the roof of the house where they choose land.

There is no rest, there are no eaves
in these decks, these landings, these so-called streets.

One year wiser, another year older,
they take one long look and pass us over.

Lady, dry your eyes and smile
because at dusk

when the sun drops out of the sky
we'll slip the latch

and drink ourselves to sleep.
And last night

as we held hands in the dark
and they tried our door,

it didn't matter that you wet yourself
with fright, because I

love you, lady, and things like that
don't change.

Remember how we idolised their names?
Remember how we dreamed

of Otterburn, and Jevington, and Buttermere?
dear God, we figured

from the top of here we would see
the curve of the earth.

And how we once wrote poetry:
about the distance

between stars, and how for some
small things

the skin on a surface of water
is bearable, impregnable.

And then at last
the long lost flat,

out of bounds
on health and safety grounds,

burgled and broken
once too often

then sealed for ages
under the staircase.

Blow its cover
like Howard Carter

and enter the tomb
of the small front room,

desecrated
and deserted

except for the presence
of a former tenant,

the infamous mummy
of Ashfield Valley,

laid to rest
in a shopping trolley, kept

under wraps
in the plastic bags

in which he was bandaged
and dumped with the garbage.

House of cards, book of the film,
story I heard, word of mouth,

son of a gun, poor in the sack,
sick in the head, close to his chest,

hand on her heart, knife in the back,
back of the hand, out of the black,

into the red, stab in the dark,
flick of the wrist, stick or twist? Twist...

see one play one, get over that,
tit for a tat, girl's best friend, snap,

chase the lady, all Jacks are wild,
one for his knob, two for a pair,

three for a prial, four on the bounce,
five on the run, bird in the bush,

ace high, low takes, double the stakes,
read 'em and weep: yours, heart, out, eat,

sign of the times, luck of the draw.
Think I'm bluffing? Start the bidding:

one for the road, ace in the hole,
both, deuce, pair, brace, two of a kind,

three for a girl, three for a crowd,
four for a boy, five for a fist,

stick or twist? Twist...six of the best,
'seventy-eight – year of the rat?

nine, ten, Joe, green, Jack the lad,
Queen of the May, King of the road,

pick of the pack, cut, call, stud, brag,
twist, twist, twist, twist, twist, bust, fold,

stack.

Light house boat house house boat dog house
mad house house keep full house hot house

house craft house style home baked in house
home front home spun home made out house

home town house hold home rule house work
guest house house guest house rule work house

house trained house maid house wife house bound
free house house fly house plant house proud

home watch guard house house call house break
home stretch home run home straight home bird

home help home truth home sick
                                          house lights.

Ashfield Valley, the tragic story
of a kissing cousin of Solomon Grundy.

Early on Monday, just after dawn
they delivered him over the drawing-board,

and on Tuesday from ten to elevenses
they opened him up with a pair of scissors,
cut the tape on a thousand homes
in his pigeonholes, in his honeycombs.

But on Wednesday at noon they called for the nurse
and at two he was bad, and at four he was worse,

and on Thursday at five an expert prescribed
an injection of cash, and the kiss of life.

But on Friday evening at twenty to nine
with boards at the windows they closed his eyes,
put him down,
read the last rites

and on Saturday night, just after dusk
it was ashes to ashes, dust to dust.

And all day Sunday, out came the people
like bees from the lion on the tin of treacle
with their beds, their bikes,
their pets and their children,

and his broken bones went to pave the way
for a business park and a motorway.

And that, as they say, was that. Well, almost,
because Ashfield Valley couldn't give up the ghost.

With his head in his hands, down but not out
he went walkabout, slouching back into town

to be drawn again,
to be born again.

Attention all shipping, attention all shipping,
to vessels in danger of demolition,
to all blocks guilty of gross dereliction.

At O seven hundred hours yesterday morning
the Met Office issued the following warning:

Ashfield. Valley. Nineteen sixty-odd
to nineteen ninety or ninety-one. And falling.

From Prestbury P and Queensbury Q
through Sandridge S to Ulverston U:

those six blocks
are now on the rocks.

For a further update of the second phase:
watch   this   space.

I don't care much
for these pooches and mutts,

and this place, you can tell from the litter they leave
has gone to the dogs, I mean literally.

How does it start? Well, how shall I put it?
You lies down with dogs, you gets up with puppies,

and only this morning I had a report in
of two dogs...how shall I say this...consorting

at midday in the corridor,
a wolfhound with a labrador

wheelbarrowing,
worrying.

No doubt about it. If you gave me a tenner
for every dog between Appleby and Zennor

I'd be rubbing shoulders with Jean Paul Getty,
or if every dog in Ashfield Valley

stood nose to tail
we'd be talking in terms of a canine chain

to Acapulco
and back again.

Oh I know the dangers, what they say
about giving a dog a bad name,

like on Otterburn a pair of pugs
I know for a fact are pushing drugs

or on Newington, an Irish setter
living over the brush with a smooth fox terrier.

And all that stuff about rottweilers,
or there again the social climbers,

dogs with ideas above their stations,
a case in point – that crowd of dalmatians –

spotted last week in the front two rows of
a tenancy meeting, looking down their noses.

and that Japanese spitz
with its satellite dish.

As for the dirt,
I'm a world expert,

the number of times I've put my foot in it,
and a gang of boxers have told me to button it

so I watch where I tread, bite my lip,
but I could write a book on it,

and let me say
on the very day

a dog moves in next door, or down below, or up above –
you mark my words, there goes the neighbourhood.

A general point
I wanted to raise
about spending time
in an enclosed place.

Whether flats or bed-sits
its all cemented
in this famous proverb
I've just invented:

the jack-in-the-box
who discovered the truth
stood up for himself
and hit the roof.

A was an Appleby, over.

Bravo Buttermere one little duck/
and veering westerly, over.

Crosshill Charlie and Delta Dunblane/
severe and rising three to four/
with Mary at the cottage door and falling, over.

Elsdon moderate. Falkirk Foxtrot five to six/
and pick up sticks increasing, over.

Granton lucky seven I require a pilot/
Hatfield one fat lady number eight and gale/
repeat gale, over.

Eyes down Irvine/
hard lines Jevington this is a warning, over.

Legs eleven Kilburn thank you whistlers what a smasher/
two fried eggs and a gammon rasher/
Langley you should stop your vessel, over.

Melbury poor, unlucky for some/
Newington poor, Otterburn poor/
and Prestbury mostly poor or falling over, over.

Seventeen eighteen/
maids in waiting Queensbury low visibility/
Romeo Rainford showers, over.

Sandridge going west to Thornhill/
fast decreasing, over.

Uniform Ulverston key to the door/
and Victor Valleyfield fading soon/
and Whisky Wentworth all filling in by noon, over.

Echo Exford, over. Exford, over. Over.

Full house Yankee Yardley dropping now/
and Zennor clearing, over.

Do you copy? Do you read me, over?

And you held up the x-ray like an Oscar –
the green light, the all clear, that 'bravo'
from the night porter sending you fox-trotting
into the gift shop: whisky for Victor,

golf balls for Charlie. Some bloody tour: the Seychelles,
India and Quebec, the Hotel Sierra for Pete's sake.
And hadn't you dreamt it – that runaway Alfa Romeo,
the slow crunch, all the sweetness of life dissolving

like sugar in hot tea which you cupped halfheartedly
saying it all in terms of swan songs and curtain calls.
But no, you were A1, OK, no pot needed.
No kilo of plaster to anchor you down

so you framed that negative – the two elegant bones –
the fibula and its friend like dance partners,
the thumbs-up, and your inhaled 'yes'
rushing off through the wards like a rumour,

its echo bouncing back to confirm it.
Clearly, you could see the comeback: London,
November, the Papa Lima Club, no feedback
in the mike, the new troupe in New York Yankee duds,

uniform then peeling to a diamond, a delta
into which you strut, that tango number
with juliet cap and cane, a knockout. Lastly
the exit, and the bitches gather on the balcony

like Zulus as you execute that double cartwheel
into the wings, over and over and out.

The pointed wind of our first winter
needles us,

it draws our breath, and patterns
on the windows.

Will this friendship splinter in these
icy times,

or can our sun-kissed history
hold us tight?

We were brilliant in the heat. Reeling
in the days

spun on the wheels of bicycles,
those summer shapes

annealed and tempered now to glimmers.
Small wonder

we're reforging old safe-keepings
for our winter.

Once, stars of coal dust deep
in the bunker,

now token things
for the electric meter.

Last night I dreamt
I sailed to Mandalay;
walked on the roof,
looked east and westward

for the sea and saw
the whole of Rochdale
as a bay
and Ashfield Valley as a cove,

deep and dark
with us in its hold
till it broke and opened
its arms and shoulders

and launched and christened us
into the ocean.
Twenty-six blocks
in this flotilla

with just one caretaker
manning the tiller.
For a thousand homes
just one captain left –

stoking the boiler,
steering this fleet
through a difficult passage
into quieter seas.

Scrubbing the landings,
clearing the decks,
the skeleton crew
of the *Marie Celeste*.

And we docked for supper,
caught and brought
a flock of flying fish
out of the sky

and killed them,
set a fire
in the engine-room
and grilled them,

souls, someone said
from the North Atlantic
of those who went down
with the S.S. *Titanic*,

the biggest, the best
and the most expensive, again
the landings, the decks
and the thousand cabins

not a million miles
from Ashfield Valley.
The rich bailed out
as we started to list,

the paint was still drying,
the band was still playing.
But with each of us safe
in our superstructures

a storm brewed up
and quickly steered us
back to Greater Manchester's
treacherous harbour;

we came alongside
and put down anchor.
Next morning the dawn
came up like thunder.

That was a dream
but over breakfast
it came back to me:
landlocked but somehow

at the same time at sea,
which at one time
was shipshape
and the place to be.

I have to say I'd never thought
of this place as a ski resort,

Ashfield Valley
and its thousand chalets,

a case of the half-light
making me snow-blind.

In any case,
this house of cards, these Meccano apartments
thirty years ago were the cat's pyjamas.

So instead
of putting the cart before the horse
I should trace this rumour back to its source;

the place: perhaps a council chamber,
the date: nineteen-sixty something or other...

CLLR APPLEBY:
>   Right then, gentlemen, matters arising:
>   picking some names for these blocks of housing.
>
>   I've had some suggestions from the Highways Department
>   such as Gracie Fields and Busby Gardens,
>
>   and I'm not impressed.
>   Gents, we need an address
>
>   that's neat and tidy, plain and simple,
>   not fancy or flash or party political,
>
>   something that folks will remember the name of
>   but not be puzzled or flummoxed or ashamed of.

CLLR BUTTERMERE:
>   This isn't as easy as some of the others,
>   there's twenty-six of these rotten buggers.

CLLR CROSSHILL:
>   Twenty-six? That couldn't be better.
>   We can start each one with a different letter;
>
>   pass me that Atlas of Britain and a pin,
>   I'll run through the sections and stick it in,
>
>   and wherever it lands, whatever it falls on,
>   that'll be the name, that's what we'll call them.

CLLR APPLEBY:
>   Great idea lad, right up my street,
>   I'm a great believer in keeping things neat.
>
>   People will know where they stand with this system,
>   so will the postman and the Gas Board and the milkman.

CLLR CROSSHILL:
    Sorry to piss on the fireworks, gents,
    but there's nothing in here beginning with X.

CLLR DUNBLANE:
    That's a blow. Still, not to worry,
    we'll pick something out of the dictionary;

    there's only a handful, I'll run through them all:
    there's Xmas, X-ray, X-the ball,

    xylophone, xenon, xanthic, xeric...
CLLR BUTTERMERE:
    It's a block of flats, not a bloody spaceship.

CLLR DUNBLANE:
    Eureka, gentlemen, this one should do,
    it's poetry or something: 'Xanadu,

    an idyllic estate or place' (and I'm quoting)
    'from *Kubla Khan* by S.T. Coleridge.'

CLLR BUTTERMERE:
    That's not a poem, it's from that song which
    Dave Dee did with Dozy, Beaky, Mick and Tich.

CLLR CROSSHILL:
    What about Exford, that's your best bet,
    it's a nice little village in Somerset

    and it's more in keeping
    with this place-name thing.

CLLR DUNBLANE:
   Exford begins with an E, not an X.

CLLR CROSSHILL:
   Oh Jesus Christ, if we're going to split hairs...

CLLR APPLEBY:
   Gentlemen, gentlemen, point of order,
   we'll take a vote; all those in favour:

   I make that six.
   Exford it is.

   A to Z. I like it, I like it.
   I don't know why nobody else hasn't tried it.

   Well, if that's O.K.
   we'll call it a day,

   and here's me thinking we'd be here till Christmas.
   Moving on then. Any other business?

Saturday night, I should step to one side.
Saturday night, a reasonable time

to sidetrack away from the beaten path,
to finish the week on a different tack.

Two steps forward, one step back.
One step forward, two steps back;

that isn't the start of some half-arsed remark
about houses and flats, not a taster of schmaltz
but tonight's first dance, a Hungarian waltz.

Left after right, right after left.
Left over right, right over left;

that's not for the sake of some sort of twist
on the best laid plans
of mice and man,
or breathing space or room to live,
not a careful dig
about places and people
but tonight's last jig, a Hungarian circle.

Fire in the hole,
let's go to town now;
raise the roof,
bring the house down.

We thought of Ashfield and imagined trees;
wood smoke, horses and the ricochet of hooves,
a meltwater stream
like milk from the moors,

beehives, bird life, allotments, a breeze.
Like bloodhounds now we track the moment of the truth,
by which I mean
the way we choose

to say which quaver tipped the song into a scream,
to pinpoint how the pinprick widened to a bruise
for you, for me.
I'll list the clues.

the so-called ash, the field, the so-called streets
at sixes, sevens, German shepherds in their schools
of threes
and twos,

for peace of mind this baseball bat, for sleep
these tablets and a certain ratio of booze
will count for sheep
and see us through.

We idle now on waiting lists, and dream
of runways, level crossings, traffic queues;
waiting to come clean,
to break the news

of how we live, of what we have seen,
of how it leaves us, and what that proves.
A light goes green,
but nobody moves.

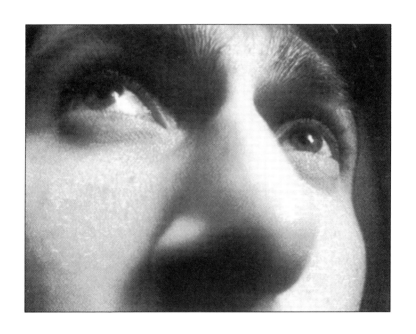

Simon Armitage was born in 1963 in Huddersfield and grew up in West Yorkshire. After taking a degree in Geography at Portsmouth Polytechnic, he worked with young offenders for two years, and then went to Manchester University, where he gained a CQSW (Certificate of Qualification in Social Work), and as part of his MA wrote a dissertation on the psychology of television violence. He now works as a probation officer in Oldham, and lives in Marsden, near Huddersfield.

He won an Eric Gregory Award in 1988. In 1989 his work was featured in Radio 3's *New Voices* series. His first book-length collection of poems *Zoom!* was published by Bloodaxe Books in 1989: it was made a Poetry Book Society Choice, was shortlisted for the Whitbread Prize and sold over 5000 copies. His second book from Bloodaxe is *Xanadu* (1992), a poem film for BBC Television from the *Words on Film* series. He has also published four pamphlets, *Human Geography* (Smith Doorstop, 1986), *The Distance Between Stars* (Wide Skirt, 1987), *The Walking Horses* (Slow Dancer Press, 1988) and *Around Robinson* (Slow Dancer Press, 1991); a cassette tape, *Zoom! and new poems* (Smith Doorstop/The Poetry Business, 1991); and another book of poems, *Kid* (Faber, 1992).